During The Sacrament It's Good To Think Of Jesus

First Edition

Printed in the United States

DURING THE SACRAMENT
it's good to think of Jesus

About the ~~line~~ Artist

Alycia Pace is an avid lover of fortune cookies,
the smell of bookstores, and movies from the 50's.
She studied Animation at BYU and served a mission
in Paris. Alycia now lives in Utah with her one year old
daughter and her husband David.

♡ fortune cookies
♡ running
♡ bookstores
♡ pulling out splinters
♡ campfires
♡ foxes
♡ thunder
♡ Gene Kelly & Doris Day

✗ football
✗ running
✗ my muffin top
✗ loud chewing
✗ wearing socks in the summer

To Learn More About Alycia Pace and Her Art Visit:

www.etsy.com/shop/PacePaintings

alyciapace.tumblr.com

and follow on instagram : PacePaintings

About the ^color Artist

_____

_____

_____

_____

write a little about yourself!

Draw a picture
of YOU!

Made in United States
Troutdale, OR
12/22/2024

27202274R00018